JOURNAL

DOING
LIFE TOGETHER

doing
life**together**

A Guided Journal by
Brett Eastman

Doing Life Together Journal
Copyright © 2005 by Brett Eastman
ISBN 0-310-81121-X

All Scripture quotations, unless otherwise noted, are taken from the *Holy Bible:
New International Version (North American Edition)*. Copyright © 1973, 1978, 1984
by International Bible Society. Used by permission of Zondervan.
All rights reserved.

Scripture quotations noted NASB are taken from the NEW AMERICAN
STANDARD BIBLE ®, © copyright The Lockman Foundation 1960, 1962, 1968, 1971,
1973, 1975, 1977. Used by permission. (www.lockman.org)

Scripture quotations noted THE MESSAGE are from *The Message: The New
Testament in Contemporary English*. Copyright © 1993 by Eugene H. Peterson.

Scripture quotations noted TLB are from *The Living Bible*, copyright © 1971.
Used by permission of Tyndale House Publishers, Inc., Wheaton, IL 60189.
All rights reserved.

The NIV and New International Version trademarks are registered in the
United States Patent and Trademark Office by International Bible Society.

All rights reserved. No part of this publication may be reproduced, stored in a
retrieval system, or transmitted in any form or by any means—electronic, mechanical,
photocopy, recording, or any other—except for brief quotations in printed reviews,
without the prior permission of the publisher.

Requests for information should be addressed to:
Inspirio, the Gift group of Zondervan
Grand Rapids, Michigan 49530
http://www.inspiriogifts.com

INTRODUCTION

The "Greatest Adventure" of our lives is simply found in the daily pursuit of knowing, growing, serving, sharing and worshipping Christ. The essence of a purposeful life is to see these five biblical purposes fully formed and in balance in our lives. It's in that balance that we achieve health, which ultimately leads to the spiritual growth we all long for as believers. It's the simple focus of Paul's words to the early church when he said to "present every man [and woman] complete in Christ" (Colossians 1:28 NASB). In order for any of us to be "complete in Christ," we need to be clear about seeing all five biblical purposes fully formed in our lives.

You and I both know this doesn't just happen. It takes a clear sense of purpose, planning, and encouragement from others. This journal is designed to give you and your group a tool to help in the process of forming Christ deep within your heart and the hearts of your people.

David poured his heart out to God in writing what we know of today as the book of Psalms. This book contains his honest conversations with God in written form. They included every imaginable emotion, and the integration of Old Testament scriptures and simple reflections on every aspect of his life.

First, I want to encourage you to carve out a few minutes to pray and plan the first steps in this journal. You can begin by reading the first story in this devotional journal on page ten and making your first entry on the Day 1 Reflections page. Then decide which of the approaches listed below you want to experiment with in reading God's Word and journaling your prayers.

This devotional journal is designed to apply the basic habits of reading God's Word and prayer in order to cultivate a more intimate walk with Christ. Let me make a few simple suggestions as you begin: As David did, select a source or strategy to integrate God's Word into your devotional time. Use any of the following resources:

- Bible
- One Year Bible
- New Testament Bible Challenge Reading Plan
- Devotional Book
- Topical Bible Study Plan

Second, before or after you read God's Word, respond back to God in honest reflection and response to His Word in the form of a written prayer. (Record this prayer in the "Reflections from my HEART" area of your journal.) You may begin this time by simply finishing the sentence: *Father... Yesterday, Lord... or Thanks, God, for...* Share with God where you are in the present moment— express your hurts, disappointments, frustrations, blessings, victories, personal wins, or reasons why you are grateful to God.

In addition to the Scripture journaling pages that are included throughout your journal, thought-provoking questions are included to help you begin thinking of ways in which you can apply God's Word in your life.

Whatever you do with your journal, set yourself up to win. You might want to share some of your progress and experiences with some or all of your group members. You may find they want to join in and even encourage you in this journey. Most of all, enjoy the ride and begin to cultivate a more authentic, growing walk with God.

Trust us on this one…This could be one of the greatest adventures of your life.

PERSONAL COVENANT

From this moment on...

I am renewing my commitment to

connect in God's family,

grow to be more like Christ,

develop my gifts for ministry,

share my life mission every day and

surrender my life for God's pleasure.

_____

Signature

_____

Date

BEGINNING
LIFE TOGETHER

GOD'S PURPOSES
FOR YOUR LIFE

My wife and I founded the church that I pastor presently. When we started the church, there were about five families who joined with us, so we were a small group among ourselves. By God's grace, this young church began to grow pretty quickly.

It grew from about 25 people to 150 people in two years. Unfortunately, right in the middle of this amazing move of God, my family experienced a great tragedy. Our youngest daughter died in her sleep one night. We were devastated. Here we were, responsible for this brand new church and surrounded by all these people that we barely knew—and we were going through the biggest crisis of our lives.

But because we had started the church with small groups, the community—the giving, the loving, the sharing—had already been built into the DNA of our young church. And although most of our new church family did not come from a religious background, they gathered around us, and they loved us. They loved us back to health over a period of time—and they did it in a way that was unlike anything that I had ever experienced in my whole life. I had grown up in the church, and I had never before felt such love. I really believe that the reason we pulled through this great tragedy was because we had developed community in our small groups. And we enjoy that to this day.

—Gary Kendall, Senior Pastor of Indian Creek Church, Kansas

1

The foundation for spiritual growth
is an intimate connection with God and his family.

What does the phrase doing life together mean to you?

What do you think of the statement, "It's often easier to love God privately than
to love the flawed people around us"?

Jesus said, "A new command I give you: Love one another. As I have loved you, so you must love one another. By this all men will know that you are my disciples, if you love one another."

JOHN 13:34–35

What's your reaction to the idea that the Christian life boils down to relationships—love for God and love for others?

How have you recently received love from God in your life? From others?

How have you recently demonstrated your love to God? To others?

DAY 1

Dear friends, since God so loved us, we also ought to love one another.

1 JOHN 4:11

Today's Scripture Passage:

Reflections from my HEART:

I *Honor* who you are. (Praise God for something.)

I *Express* who I'm not. (Confess any known sin.)

I *Affirm* who I am in you. (How does God see you?)

I *Request* your will for me. (Ask God for something.)

I *Thank* you for what you've done. (Thank God for something.)

JOURNAL DAY 2

2

Love involves faithfully showing up,
encouraging each other, and motivating each other
to do good deeds.

Think of a time when you felt encouraged. Did someone say or do something to make you feel that way

Think of a time when you were discouraged by another person. What did that person say or do to make you feel that way?

Let us hold unswervingly
to the hope we profess,
for he who promised is
faithful. And let us con-
sider how we may spur
one another on toward
love and good deeds.

HEBREWS 10:23–24

Have you discouraged anyone lately? If so, how? What can you do to make the situation right?

How have you been an encourager lately?

List three people you can encourage in the next week—and how you plan to do so.

DAY
2

Let us encourage one another—and all the more as you see the Day approaching. **HEBREWS 10:25**

_____

_____

_____

_____

_____

_____

_____

_____

_____

_____

_____

_____

_____

_____

_____

_____

Today's Scripture Passage:

Reflections from my HEART:

I *Honor* who you are. (Praise God for something.)
I *Express* who I'm not. (Confess any known sin.)
I *Affirm* who I am in you. (How does God see you?)
I *Request* your will for me. (Ask God for something.)
I *Thank* you for what you've done. (Thank God for something.)

DAY
2

_____
_____
_____
_____
_____
_____
_____
_____
_____
_____
_____
_____
_____
_____
_____
_____
_____
_____
_____

In order to be spiritually fruitful,
we need to do whatever it takes to stay connected
to Jesus Christ, our true vine.

In practical, day-to-day terms, how have you "made your home"
with Jesus Christ?

In what ways do you need to reconnect with Christ, the true vine?

3

JOURNAL DAY 3

Jesus said, "Live in me.
Make your home in me
just as I do in you."

—**JOHN 15:5**
THE MESSAGE

What fruit have been displayed in your life as a result of your relationship with Jesus? (If you need to, take a look at the fruit of the Spirit listed in Galatians 5:22–23.)

What are some things that have hindered you in bearing fruit for Christ? How can you eliminate those things from your Christian walk?

DAY 3

See that what you have heard from the beginning remains in you. If it does, you also will remain in the Son and in the Father. **1 JOHN 2:24**

Today's Scripture Passage:

Reflections from my HEART:

I *Honor* who you are. (Praise God for something.)
I *Express* who I'm not. (Confess any known sin.)
I *Affirm* who I am in you. (How does God see you?)
I *Request* your will for me. (Ask God for something.)
I *Thank* you for what you've done. (Thank God for something.)

DAY 3

_____

_____

_____

_____

_____

_____

_____

_____

_____

_____

_____

_____

_____

_____

_____

JOURNAL DAY 3

3

Serving God by doing something he wants done is a way of expressing your love for him.

Describe some of the talents and resources God has entrusted to you.

How has your love for God motivated you to serve His kingdom and serve other people?

Describe a time in your life when you successfully used one of your talents for God's glory.

Jesus said, "Well done, good and faithful servant! You have been faithful with a few things; I will put you in charge of many things. Come and share your master's happiness!"

MATTHEW 25:21

Describe a time when you failed to use one of your talents. What caused you to fall short? What can you do differently in the future?

Close your eyes and picture Jesus saying the following words to you: "Well done, My good and faithful servant." What feelings and emotions does this visualization bring to the surface?

List some areas of service in which you are currently involved. What are some areas of service in which you would like to become more active? What will you do to become more involved in these areas?

DAY
3

Each one should use whatever gift he has received to serve others, faithfully administering God's grace in its various forms.

1 PETER 4:10

*life***together**
DOING

Today's Scripture Passage:

Reflections from my HEART:

I *Honor* who you are. (Praise God for something.)
I *Express* who I'm not. (Confess any known sin.)
I *Affirm* who I am in you. (How does God see you?)
I *Request* your will for me. (Ask God for something.)
I *Thank* you for what you've done. (Thank God for something.)

_____

_____

_____

_____

_____

_____

_____

_____

_____

_____

_____

_____

_____

_____

_____

_____

_____

4

"Preach the gospel at all times.
When necessary, use words."
—Francis of Assisi

How have you recently been a shining light for Christ in the darkness of the world? Be specific.

Have you ever known someone who accepted Christ because of the actions of a believer? What drew that person to the Savior?

Jesus said, "Let your light shine before men, that they may see your good deeds and praise your Father in heaven."

MATTHEW 5:16

Have you ever known someone who rejected Christ because of the actions of a believer? Explain. How can you prevent this from happening in your own Christian walk?

What things in your life make "shining your light" more challenging? What can you do to be a light despite these challenges?

Who are the people who most need to see Jesus shining through you? What are some practical ways to reach them with His love?

DAY 4

Live such good lives among the pagans that…they may see your good deeds and glorify God. **1 PETER 2:12**

_____

_____

_____

_____

_____

_____

_____

_____

_____

_____

_____

_____

_____

_____

_____

_____

_____

_____

Today's Scripture Passage:

Reflections from my HEART:

I *Honor* who you are. (Praise God for something.)

I *Express* who I'm not. (Confess any known sin.)

I *Affirm* who I am in you. (How does God see you?)

I *Request* your will for me. (Ask God for something.)

I *Thank* you for what you've done. (Thank God for something.)

5

Life together with God and his family
ultimately leads us to surrender ourselves wholly to God.

What does the word surrender mean to you? Does it have good or bad
connotations? Why?

What is the relationship between surrender and trust? How might trust be a
factor in how much—or how little—you surrender to God?

Submit yourselves,
then, to God.

JAMES 4:7

What areas of your life are easier for you to surrender to God?
Which areas are more difficult? Why do you suppose this is?

How does surrendering all of your life to God affect your relationships
with other members of God's family?

Write a prayer of surrender to God below. Include areas that you are
struggling to turn over to him. Thank him for his grace that enables
you to turn everything over to his care.

**DAY
5**

_____

_____

_____

_____

_____

_____

_____

_____

_____

> "I tell you the truth," Jesus
> said, "no one who has left
> home or wife or brothers or
> parents or children for the
> sake of the kingdom of God
> will fail to receive many
> times as much in this age
> and, in the age to come,
> eternal life."
>
> **LUKE 18:29–30**

Today's Scripture Passage:

Reflections from my HEART:

I *Honor* who you are. (Praise God for something.)
I *Express* who I'm not. (Confess any known sin.)
I *Affirm* who I am in you. (How does God see you?)
I *Request* your will for me. (Ask God for something.)
I *Thank* you for what you've done. (Thank God for something.)

DAY

5

CONNECTING WITH GOD'S FAMILY

FELLOWSHIP

On the very first evening of our group, I became really excited about the amount

of sharing and transparency that was taking place. But there was one man who

was sitting off to the side, kind of quiet. He had come to our group from a

different church, and I didn't know him.

Near the end of the meeting, he looked up and said, "There is just one thing that

I want to share with you. This is the very first church activity I've been to in over

four years." When I asked him why, he said, "Over four years ago, I got mad at

God because my son was killed." Silence filled the room. All of a sudden,

another man looked up at the first man with tears in his eyes and said,

"The reason you were brought to this group is because six years ago, my son was killed.

Maybe we're here just to share our experiences with each other."

These two men have now bonded and become friends, and they meet together

and pray together regularly. It's been an amazing thing.

—Bob Palocsay

6

The more aware we are of who we really are,
the more Jesus is able to connect with us
and the more we are able to connect with others.

When was the first time you became aware of God's desire to connect with you?
How did you respond?

What does the phrase, *"It is not the healthy who need a doctor, but the sick,"* mean
to you?

Describe a time when you were "sick" but you responded to Jesus' call.

Jesus said, "It is not
the healthy who need a
doctor, but the sick.... I
have not come to call
the righteous but sin-
ners."

MATTHEW 9:12–13

In what ways has Jesus made you "healthy" since you began to follow him?

List two or three specific ways Jesus has asked you to follow him. Have you been obedient? Why or why not?

Describe the difference that following Christ has made in your life.

DAY 6

"Come, follow me," Jesus said.

MATTHEW 4:19

Today's Scripture Passage:

Reflections from my HEART:

I *Honor* who you are. (Praise God for something.)
I *Express* who I'm not. (Confess any known sin.)
I *Affirm* who I am in you. (How does God see you?)
I *Request* your will for me. (Ask God for something.)
I *Thank* you for what you've done. (Thank God for something.)

DAY 6

7

The more securely we know God as the lover of our souls, the more we will be able to sustain close connections with other human beings.

"We love to the degree that we are truly convinced we are loved." Do you agree or disagree with this statement? Why?

Are you truly convinced of God's love for you? If not, what is standing in the way?

No one has ever seen God; but if we love one another, God lives in us and his love is made complete in us.

1 JOHN 4:12

How has experiencing God's love inspired you to love other people? Be specific.

How has God's love been "made complete" in you this week?

List five tangible ways you can express the love you have received from God to the people around you.

Now that you have purified yourselves by obeying the truth so that you have sincere love for your brothers, love one another deeply, from the heart. **1 PETER 1:22**

DAY
7

Today's Scripture Passage:

Reflections from my HEART:

I *Honor* who you are. (Praise God for something.)
I *Express* who I'm not. (Confess any known sin.)
I *Affirm* who I am in you. (How does God see you?)
I *Request* your will for me. (Ask God for something.)
I *Thank* you for what you've done. (Thank God for something.)

DAY
7

Ordinary people become extraordinary
as they live in a community founded on God's love.

Are you a person who shares yourself easily with others, or do you tend to hold back? Why?

What would a "sharing community" look like to you?

All the believers met together constantly and shared everything with each other.

ACTS 2:44 TLB

How would true fellowship within the Church have an impact on the greater community and society at large?

The word for "fellowship" in the Greek is koin_nia, and it implies a sharing and commonality among believers. How have you experienced koin_nia in your church family?

What can you, as an individual, do to encourage and strengthen the koin_nia in your church community?

DAY 8

Be devoted to one another in brotherly love...Share with God's people who are in need. **ROMANS 12:10, 13**

Today's Scripture Passage:

Reflections from my HEART:

I *Honor* who you are. (Praise God for something.)
I *Express* who I'm not. (Confess any known sin.)
I *Affirm* who I am in you. (How does God see you?)
I *Request* your will for me. (Ask God for something.)
I *Thank* you for what you've done. (Thank God for something.)

DAY 8

_____

_____

_____

_____

_____

_____

_____

_____

_____

_____

_____

_____

9

True fellowship with other believers involves authenticity, transparency, honesty, and vulnerability.

Consider what authentic, honest relationships with God and other people would look like. How can this be compared with "walking in the light"?

What does honesty in relationships mean to you?

If we walk in the light, as he is in the light, we have fellowship with one another.

1 JOHN 1:7

Is it easy or difficult for you to be transparent in your relationship with God? With other people? Why?

Can there ever be such a thing as too much honesty? Explain your answer.

List any personal risks you see in being honest about your weaknesses in a community of caring Christians. Describe how the rewards of such vulnerability might outweigh these risks.

> Confess your sins to each other and pray for each other so that you may be healed. **JAMES 5:16**

DAY 9

_____

_____

_____

_____

_____

_____

_____

_____

_____

_____

_____

_____

_____

_____

_____

_____

_____

_____

Today's Scripture Passage:

Reflections from my HEART:

I *Honor* who you are. (Praise God for something.)
I *Express* who I'm not. (Confess any known sin.)
I *Affirm* who I am in you. (How does God see you?)
I *Request* your will for me. (Ask God for something.)
I *Thank* you for what you've done. (Thank God for something.)

DAY
9

10

As you learn to use conflict productively,
you will become a tool in God's hand,
a tool that sharpens others without harming them.

How do you feel about conflict with other people? Uncertain? Frightened?
Uncomfortable? Or are you comfortable with managing conflict? What makes
you feel this way?

List some ways in which it is possible to be angry, and yet, not sin. Provide examples from your own experience.

> "In your anger do not sin": Do not let the sun go down while you are still angry, and do not give the devil a foothold.
>
> **EPHESIANS 4:26–27**

List some ways in which it is possible to "give the devil a foothold" in your anger. Has this ever happened to you? If so, what was the situation, and how was it resolved?

Has there ever been a time when conflict seemed to "sharpen" you, like "iron"? Describe the time. In what ways were you sharpened?

What conflicts are currently taking place in your life? How might they be resolved in a godly way?

DAY 10

As iron sharpens iron, so one man sharpens another.

PROVERBS 27:17

Today's Scripture Passage:

Reflections from my HEART:

I *Honor* who you are. (Praise God for something.)
I *Express* who I'm not. (Confess any known sin.)
I *Affirm* who I am in you. (How does God see you?)
I *Request* your will for me. (Ask God for something.)
I *Thank* you for what you've done. (Thank God for something.)

DAY 10

JOURNAL DAY 11

11

Christian community is not an ideal,
but a reality we can experience only in Jesus Christ.

Dietrich Bonhoeffer declared that we are "privileged to live in visible fellowship with other Christians," for "the physical presence of other Christians is a source of incomparable joy and strength to the believer."1 What do you think it means to "live in visible fellowship" with other believers?

How has the physical presence of other Christians around you drawn you closer to Christ himself?

Many, O LORD my God,
are the wonders you
have done. The things
you planned for us no
one can recount to you;
were I to speak and tell
of them, they would be
too many to declare.

PSALM 40:5

Have you been inspired recently by the testimony of another Christian? What has their story meant to you?

In what meaningful, relevant ways can you share God's faithfulness—"tell of his wonders"—with other Christians around you?

Write out a brief testimony of something God has done for you recently. List two or three people with whom you can share your story this week.

I will praise you, O LORD, with all my heart;
I will tell of all your wonders. **PSALM 9:1**

DAY
11

Today's Scripture Passage:

Reflections from my HEART:

I *Honor* who you are. (Praise God for something.)
I *Express* who I'm not. (Confess any known sin.)
I *Affirm* who I am in you. (How does God see you?)
I *Request* your will for me. (Ask God for something.)
I *Thank* you for what you've done. (Thank God for something.)

DAY
11

I would like to tell you about a success story in our small group. There was a single young lady in our group who worked for the EMT service. About a year ago, she was involved in a horrible accident. The ambulance she was in flipped five or six times, and she was in really bad shape.

Since that time, she has been going through recovery. She's had to go through lots of therapy physically, but it's the mental battle that has been the biggest challenge for her. She's been told she'll never be able to work as an EMT again—and this was a career that she loved. She has done this work all of her professional life. But what's been really great is that in our small group, she has been able to share these feelings, the hurt and the pain that she is experiencing. And what has been so refreshing to see is how our small group has come to her side and encouraged her and loved her during this time. Because of this love and support, we've watched her change into an almost different person. She became bright; she was happy; she began to have a positive outlook on what the Lord has done in her life.

She recently had to have major surgery to fuse a couple of disks in order to relieve some of the ongoing pain she was having. I decided to stop by one day after work to visit her in the hospital. Much to my surprise, when I showed up—this delighted me beyond belief— there were already four members of our small group in the hospital room visiting with her! She was in a lot of pain, and on a lot of medication, but the look on her face was amazing. She knew that these people cared for her and loved her, and she told each of us specifically how much our visit meant to her—and it was real.

Other than explaining it to you this way, you just have to be a part of something like that for yourself to understand what it's like. I know that these are lifelong friendships and relationships that are being forged in our group. Right now, it is my friend who needs our love and support, but one day it could be me or someone in my family. And the group will be there for me.

—Jeff May

GROWING TO BE
LIKE CHRIST

DISCIPLESHIP

Five years ago, I experienced a time in my career when I was discouraged and facing the toughest crisis I'd faced in my whole life. People at work had let me down, and my relationship with God was on shaky ground. I seemed to be facing stress everywhere I turned—at work, in my family, in my walk with God—and I was asking a lot of "Why me?" questions. Finally I began to ask God for a new work environment, and in the midst of that he began to show me creative ideas for my career, which is in computer work. Ultimately he called me back to the things I had been doing originally, in his original call on my life. Out of that difficult time in my life came a God-given idea for an Internet tool that would be very helpful to churches.

John 12:24 says that if a kernel of wheat falls to the ground and dies, it can produce many seeds. In my walk with God, my discipleship process, I had to die to who I thought I was. But out of that death and brokenness came new life, and a new idea that I'm now beginning to see multiply and become a blessing for many other people. What an incredible joy! Now when I look back at that difficult and broken time in my life, I am filled with gratitude—gratitude that God walked me through it, and that he had a purpose to use it for his glory.

—Boyd Pelley

12

If you really want to know Jesus Christ intimately, it takes time, energy, and the decision to let the Holy Spirit be in control of your life.

What does the term *spiritual growth* mean to you? In your mind, what are the essential elements of "growing in Christ"?

In what ways have you persevered in your spiritual walk? In what areas do you need to persevere further?

Since we are surrounded by such a great cloud of witnesses, let us throw off everything that hinders and the sin that so easily entangles, and let us run with perseverance the race marked out for us.

HEBREWS 12:1

What hindrances—outright sins, or other distractions—have prevented you from running a disciplined race for Jesus Christ? Write a prayer to God asking for His forgiveness and help to remain focused on the prize.

How does the joy of knowing Jesus intimately help to motivate your spiritual growth?

What specific, practical things can you do over the next six months to spur your spiritual growth on to a higher level? Write a statement of commitment to the Lord to persevere in these areas.

DAY

12

I have fought the good fight, I have finished the race, I have kept the faith. Now there is in store for me the crown of righteousness, which the Lord, the righteous Judge, will award to me on that day—and not only to me, but also to all who have longed for his appearing.

2 TIMOTHY 4:7–8

Today's Scripture Passage:

Reflections from my HEART:

I *Honor* who you are. (Praise God for something.)
I *Express* who I'm not. (Confess any known sin.)
I *Affirm* who I am in you. (How does God see you?)
I *Request* your will for me. (Ask God for something.)
I *Thank* you for what you've done. (Thank God for something.)

_____
_____
_____
_____
_____
_____
_____
_____
_____
_____
_____
_____
_____
_____
_____
_____

13

If you want to become complete in Jesus Christ, you'll have to let the Holy Spirit do some serious work in your life. You can't do it alone. You have to daily choose to depend on the Holy Spirit.

With what "deeds of the flesh" do you still struggle? Make a list, and then write a prayer to God, asking the Holy Spirit to help you overcome your flesh and walk fully in the Spirit.

List the fruits of the Spirit (found in Galatians 5:22–23) in the order of their prominence in your life. Which ones are the highest and lowest? Why?

The fruit of the Spirit is love, joy, peace, patience, kindness, goodness, faithfulness, gentleness and self-control. Against such things there is no law. Those who belong to Christ Jesus have crucified the sinful nature with its passions and desires. Since we live by the Spirit, let us keep in step with the Spirit.

GALATIANS 5:22–25

What does it mean to "walk by the Spirit"?

Describe a recent temptation you have faced. Did you rely on the Holy Spirit to help you resist this temptation? Why or why not?

List some practical ways in which you can rely on the Holy Spirit for help over the next week.

So I say, live by the Spirit.

GALATIANS 5:16

DAY

13

Today's Scripture Passage:

Reflections from my HEART:

I *Honor* who you are. (Praise God for something.)
I *Express* who I'm not. (Confess any known sin.)
I *Affirm* who I am in you. (How does God see you?)
I *Request* your will for me. (Ask God for something.)
I *Thank* you for what you've done. (Thank God for something.)

DAY
13

God longs to cultivate a deep relationship with you.
He jealously seeks those who will seek him.

14

What motivates you to spend time in God's presence?

Do you ever have trouble maintaining a personal quiet time with God?
What obstacles most often stand in your way?

What can you do to eliminate some of these obstacles?

O God, you are my God,
earnestly I seek you;
my soul thirsts for you,
my body longs for you,
in a dry and weary land
where there is no water.

PSALM 63:1

Have you ever experienced a time when you have longed for God as a dying man longs for water in a dry and thirsty land? What was unique about that time?

Write a prayer of commitment to the Lord, to begin or maintain a personal quiet time alone with him. Describe for him why you enjoy spending time with him.

<table>
<tr><td>DAY
14</td><td>"Come, all you who are thirsty, come to the waters," says the LORD... "Listen, listen to me, and eat what is good, and your soul will delight in the richest of fare. Give ear and come to me; hear me, that your soul may live." ISAIAH 55:1–3</td></tr>
</table>

TIPS FOR A FRUITFUL
PERSONAL TIME WITH GOD

1. Set a definite time—a time when you will be most alert.

2. Choose a quiet place—a place where you won't be disturbed.

3. Start out with just ten or fifteen minutes.

4. Include Bible reading, prayer, and confession of any sin you're aware of.

5. Be habitual about it; it takes about six weeks to develop a new habit.

6. Determine ahead of time what you are going to do.

7. Be creative; consider varying the things you do during your quiet time (Bible reading, listening to a worship CD, journaling your praise to God, meditating on a single verse or passage of Scripture).

8. Write down in your journal what you are learning about God and what you believe he wants you to do (submit to correction, respond in a specific act of obedience, offer him praise, accept his forgiveness, bow before him in repentance).

Today's Scripture Passage:

Reflections from my HEART:

I *Honor* who you are. (Praise God for something.)
I *Express* who I'm not. (Confess any known sin.)
I *Affirm* who I am in you. (How does God see you?)
I *Request* your will for me. (Ask God for something.)
I *Thank* you for what you've done. (Thank God for something.)

DAY

14

God knows your name and your thoughts, your joys and your challenges. He simply loves you in the midst of your weaknesses, and he desires a growing friendship with you.

15

We develop our friendship with God through prayer. Do you find prayer to be part of a meaningful relationship with God, or a tedious exercise to be endured? What makes you feel this way?

What are some challenges you are currently facing in your prayer life? What are some practical ways you can overcome these challenges?

Jesus said, "When you pray, go into your room, close the door and pray to your Father, who is unseen. Then your Father, who sees what is done in secret, will reward you.

MATTHEW 6:6

Write out a prayer to God using the following prompts from the Lord's Prayer:

Dear Father who… (Write something about God that you marvel at. This is called praise, worship, honor, adoration.)
I so much want to see that your will is done in the area of…
Please give me and those I love… (Write things you'd like God to do for you or for others. This is called supplication, intercession, or just plain asking for help!)

DAY 15

Do not be anxious about anything, but in everything, by prayer and petition, with thanksgiving, present your requests to God. **PHILIPPIANS 4:6**

Forgive me for... (Write down any items you need to clear up with God.
This is called confession.)

I forgive... (Any grudges to let go of?)
Please protect me or others from...
Thank you, Father!

_____

_____

_____

_____

_____

_____

_____

_____

_____

_____

_____

_____

_____

_____

_____

_____

_____

_____

Today's Scripture Passage:

Reflections from my HEART:

I *Honor* who you are. (Praise God for something.)
I *Express* who I'm not. (Confess any known sin.)
I *Affirm* who I am in you. (How does God see you?)
I *Request* your will for me. (Ask God for something.)
I *Thank* you for what you've done. (Thank God for something.)

DAY
15

If you spend time in personal study of God's Word, you will be blessed, approved by God, stable, successful, and prosperous.

What place does Bible study hold in your life today?

How easy or difficult is it for you to study the Scriptures? Why do you believe this is?

16

JOURNAL DAY 16

The law of the LORD is perfect, reviving the soul. The statutes of the LORD are trustworthy, making wise the simple. The precepts of the LORD are right, giving joy to the heart. The commands of the LORD are radiant, giving light to the eyes.

PSALM 19:7–8

When faced with a major decision, how often do you turn to the Bible for guidance?

How often do you turn to other sources first (family members, friends, colleagues, books, magazines, or other resources)?

DAY
16

Your word is a lamp to my feet and a light for my path.

PSALM 119:105

Describe a time when you used the Word of God to help you through a situation.

Now describe a time when you did not.

What were the primary differences in these two situations?

What can you learn from these situations to help you look to God's Word in the future?

I have hidden your word in my heart, O Lord, that I might not sin against you.

PSALM 119:11

DAY
16

_____

_____

_____

_____

_____

_____

_____

_____

_____

_____

_____

_____

_____

_____

_____

_____

_____

_____

Today's Scripture Passage:

Reflections from my HEART:

I *Honor* who you are. (Praise God for something.)
I *Express* who I'm not. (Confess any known sin.)
I *Affirm* who I am in you. (How does God see you?)
I *Request* your will for me. (Ask God for something.)
I *Thank* you for what you've done. (Thank God for something.)

DAY
16

_____

_____

_____

_____

_____

_____

_____

_____

_____

_____

_____

_____

_____

_____

_____

_____

_____

17

The storms of life can sometimes feel like hurricanes,
but without such times of turmoil and hardship,
we would not bear fruit.

Have there been any trials in your life that you were not able to endure joyfully?
Why were they so difficult?

How might an outlook of joy have made these trials easier to bear?

Consider it pure joy,
my brothers, whenever
you face trials of many
kinds, because you
know that the testing
of your faith develops
perseverance.

JAMES 1:2–3

How is your character and walk with God different because of the trials you have come through?

What trials are you currently facing?

How might the lessons you have learned in past circumstances help you face your current trials with joy?

DAY 17

Dear friends, do not be surprised at the painful trial you are suffering, as though something strange were happening to you. But rejoice that you participate in the sufferings of Christ, so that you may be overjoyed when his glory is revealed. **1 PETER 4:12–13**

_____
_____
_____
_____
_____
_____
_____
_____
_____
_____
_____
_____
_____
_____
_____
_____
_____
_____
_____
_____

Today's Scripture Passage:

Reflections from my HEART:

I *Honor* who you are. (Praise God for something.)
I *Express* who I'm not. (Confess any known sin.)
I *Affirm* who I am in you. (How does God see you?)
I *Request* your will for me. (Ask God for something.)
I *Thank* you for what you've done. (Thank God for something.)

DAY 17

DEVELOPING YOUR SHAPE TO SERVE OTHERS

MINISTRY

Our group got together and decided it was time for us to serve, to do a food drive to glorify God, and do it in a way that no one else had. We stood outside of grocery stores with red bags and a short list, and handed them out to people who were going into the store, asking them to purchase and then donate the items on the list. People would go into the store, shop for the items, put them in the red bag, and then give them to us, and we would take all of the food to a local outreach at the end of the day. We made it easy for people to give, and God moved on so many people's hearts in amazing ways. At the end of our first food drive, we had collected two-and-a-half-tons of food, enough for 116,000 meals—in only one day of service. At the last drive, we had 260 people serving at twenty-three different grocery stores, and we collected thirty-three tons of food in a single day. This was nothing we could have planned on our own—God definitely had his hand in it.

I want to share one story. One man called and wanted to serve because he had been on the streets himself at one time. Here's a guy who wanted to serve because he'd been homeless, and he had to take a bus for fifteen miles to get to the grocery store. It took him three hours of travel time in order to be able to serve for four hours.

Serving God in this way has made significant changes in my life. Now, whenever I get caught up in the rat race, I plan a food drive. It gets me centered back on the things that are important, focused on God. When we're out there serving, people get curious about why we're doing what we're doing, and it lights a fire inside of them. It's our way of witnessing, getting them to step back and think about what they can do to help others.

—Greg Weinstein

All your physical attributes, your personality, the way you think, your experiences, your passions, your abilities, and even your failures make up the unique person you are. You are God's masterpiece!

What things about yourself do you like the most?

What things about yourself are the hardest to accept?

How do you see these things—both good and bad—as a part of God's plan for your life?

> I praise you because
> I am fearfully and
> wonderfully made;
> your works are
> wonderful,
> I know that full well.
>
> **PSALM 139:14**

What "good works" have you done for God recently?

For what "good works"—to be done both now and in the future—do you believe God has created you?

In what ways is God preparing you now to do these good works for him in the future?

DAY
18

We are God's workmanship, created in Christ Jesus to do good works, which God prepared in advance for us to do. **EPHESIANS 2:10**

_____

_____

_____

_____

_____

_____

_____

_____

_____

_____

_____

_____

_____

_____

_____

_____

_____

_____

Today's Scripture Passage:

Reflections from my HEART:

I *Honor* who you are. (Praise God for something.)
I *Express* who I'm not. (Confess any known sin.)
I *Affirm* who I am in you. (How does God see you?)
I *Request* your will for me. (Ask God for something.)
I *Thank* you for what you've done. (Thank God for something.)

19

A servant's heart doesn't come naturally to any of us. The willingness to set aside our own agendas is essential for learning how God wants us to use our abilities.

Is it easy or difficult for you to serve others? Why do you think this is?

When you think about becoming "great" in this world, what sorts of things do you picture for yourself? How does your mindset reflect the definition of greatness Jesus gave in Mark 10:43–44?

Jesus said, "Whoever wants to be great among you must be your servant, and whoever wants to be first must be slave of all. For even the Son of Man did not come to be served, but to serve, and to give his life as a ransom for many."

MARK 10:43–45

What does it mean to you to "consider others better than yourself"?
How have you displayed this attitude recently?

How might you have behaved in a selfish or un-Christlike manner recently?
Write a prayer asking for God's forgiveness and the desire to serve others unselfishly.

List some tangible acts of servanthood you can perform this week.
How will you carry them out?

Do nothing out of selfish ambition or vain conceit, but in humility consider others better than yourselves. Each of you should look not only to your own interests, but also to the interests of others. **PHILIPPIANS 2:3–4**

DAY
19

Today's Scripture Passage:

Reflections from my HEART:

I *Honor* who you are. (Praise God for something.)
I *Express* who I'm not. (Confess any known sin.)
I *Affirm* who I am in you. (How does God see you?)
I *Request* your will for me. (Ask God for something.)
I *Thank* you for what you've done. (Thank God for something.)

DAY
19

20

Not one of us has the right to be either arrogant or
embarrassed about the gifts God has given us.
God has designed each of us differently
to reflect the many parts of him.

What spiritual gifts do you feel God has blessed you with?
(If necessary, refer to Romans 12:3–8; 1 Corinthians 12:1–11, 27–31;
Ephesians 4:11–12; and 1 Peter 4:9–11.)

In what ways are you currently using these gifts in the kingdom of God?

There are different
kinds of gifts, but the
same Spirit. There are
different kinds of
service, but the
same Lord.

1 CORINTHIANS 12:4–5

The apostle Paul often compares the Christian community to a human body. What comparisons do you see between your own particular gifts and a human body?

In what new areas could you begin to serve according to the gifts God has given you?

Write a prayer of commitment to God, thanking him for the gifts he has given to you, and pledging to honor him with those gifts in the service of others.

DAY 20

Just as each of us has one body with many members, and these members do not all have the same function, so in Christ we who are many form one body, and each member belongs to all the others. We have different gifts, according to the grace given us. **ROMANS 12:4–6**

Today's Scripture Passage:

Reflections from my HEART:

I *Honor* who you are. (Praise God for something.)
I *Express* who I'm not. (Confess any known sin.)
I *Affirm* who I am in you. (How does God see you?)
I *Request* your will for me. (Ask God for something.)
I *Thank* you for what you've done. (Thank God for something.)

DAY 20

_____

_____

_____

_____

_____

_____

_____

_____

_____

_____

_____

_____

_____

_____

21

Any personality trait can be a weakness or a strength, depending on whether it has been surrendered to God and purified in the fire of the Holy Spirit.

Briefly describe your personality. Are you an extrovert or an introvert? Do you like routine or variety? Are you self-controlled or expressive? Cooperative or competitive?

Are there any parts of your personality that you wish you could change? How might realizing that God created you as a unique individual help to accept these things about yourself?

God, who set me apart from birth and called me by his grace, was pleased to reveal his Son in me.

GALATIANS 1:15–16

In what ways is Jesus revealed through your personality?

What parts of your personality still need to be surrendered to the control of the Holy Spirit?

How might these "negative" aspects of your personality be turned to God's glory and the service of others when they are surrendered to him?

I remind you to fan into flame the gift of God.

2 TIMOTHY 1:6

DAY
21

_____

_____

_____

_____

_____

_____

_____

_____

_____

_____

_____

_____

_____

_____

_____

_____

_____

_____

_____

Today's Scripture Passage:

Reflections from my HEART:

I *Honor* who you are. (Praise God for something.)
I *Express* who I'm not. (Confess any known sin.)
I *Affirm* who I am in you. (How does God see you?)
I *Request* your will for me. (Ask God for something.)
I *Thank* you for what you've done. (Thank God for something.)

DAY
21

22

Our experiences of failure, sin, betrayal, or violation can become fruitful when we surrender them to God.

What is a painful experience that you have been through, but which you have seen work out for the good, either for yourself or for someone else?

Have you ever had an experience that seemed impossible for God to redeem for good? Explain.

We know that in all things God works for the good of those who love him, who have been called according to his purpose.

ROMANS 8:28

How have the past trials and experiences of someone else helped you through a time of difficulty in your life?

What trials or problems are you experiencing right now?

How have the past—and present—experiences in your life qualified you to help other people in similar situations?

DAY 22

Joseph said to his brothers, "You intended to harm me, but God intended it for good to accomplish what is now being done, the saving of many lives."

GENESIS 50:20

Today's Scripture Passage:

Reflections from my HEART:

I *Honor* who you are. (Praise God for something.)
I *Express* who I'm not. (Confess any known sin.)
I *Affirm* who I am in you. (How does God see you?)
I *Request* your will for me. (Ask God for something.)
I *Thank* you for what you've done. (Thank God for something.)

_____
_____
_____
_____
_____
_____
_____
_____
_____
_____
_____
_____

23

Your heart is the core of you—
the center of your desires, motives, feelings, attitudes,
and inclinations.

When you feel passionate about something God feels passionate about,
you have a strong clue that it's something you should pursue.
What are the things that you are passionate about?
What stirs up righteous anger within you or gives you great joy?

How do you "delight yourself in the LORD" on a daily basis?
How has this changed the desires of your heart?

Delight yourself in
the LORD and he
will give you the
desires of your heart.

PSALM 37:4

How have you used your passions to serve the kingdom of God?
What has been the result?

What are some areas in which you could further tap into the passionate
desires of your heart in order to advance God's kingdom?

Write a prayer to God, surrendering your passions and your heart's deepest desires
to him. Ask him to help you serve him through these strong feelings and desires.

> Christ! No more, no less. That's what I'm working so hard at day after day,
> year after year, doing my best with the energy God so generously gives me.
>
> **COLOSSIANS 1:28–29 THE MESSAGE**

DAY 23

_____

_____

_____

_____

_____

_____

_____

_____

_____

_____

_____

_____

_____

_____

_____

_____

_____

_____

Today's Scripture Passage:

Reflections from my HEART:

I *Honor* who you are. (Praise God for something.)
I *Express* who I'm not. (Confess any known sin.)
I *Affirm* who I am in you. (How does God see you?)
I *Request* your will for me. (Ask God for something.)
I *Thank* you for what you've done. (Thank God for something.)

DAY
23

One of the dangers of being authentic and serving in an authentic ministry where you talk

about real-life stuff—where you rip off some scabs and open some closet doors—is that

all of a sudden reality can come in and run headlong into your faith. Sometimes I try to

keep those two things separate, but God wants them to be together—and that can be scary,

and it can be really, really hard. So when people in the group start talking about life and

marriage problems and divorce and depression and dysfunctional families—all the things

that are really real—it can be difficult to merge reality with faith. As a group leader,

at first I thought I was supposed to have all of the answers, but I have learned that people

aren't really looking for answers. They are just looking for someone who understands

what they're going through. That's what ministry is: telling someone they're not alone.

When they can look across the room and find that you're struggling in your marriage, too,

they know they're not alone. When Jesus says to us, "You're not alone," that's what most

people are looking for. They're not looking to learn five ways to make my marriage better,

or three steps to raising perfect kids—what they're looking for is to hear:

"You don't have to go through this by yourself!"

—Jim Burgen

SHARING YOUR LIFE
MISSION EVERY DAY

EVANGELISM

Years ago, I was in business in Scottsdale, Arizona: I was an alcoholic who owned a bar.
My wife had grown up in church, but she had never accepted Christ as her personal Savior.
We ended up buying a house in Phoenix—right next door to a "Jesus freak."
This woman kept evangelizing and witnessing to my wife, until finally my wife received
Christ—and then the two of them began dropping gospel pamphlets around the house.
Around that time, life started getting bad for me. I didn't like who I'd become,
and I didn't like what I was doing for a living.

Finally, one Christmas Eve, I asked my wife, "You really believe this stuff you've been
leaving around the house?" When she said yes, I knew I needed a change, and so I prayed
the prayer of salvation. Jesus Christ came into my heart, and my life began to change.
God began to intervene, and my wife and I started serving him. We ended up with a
small Bible study in our home on Sunday evenings. I wondered at times why people
would listen to me—only three years ago I was a drunk. But because of a nosy neighbor
who wouldn't give up, our lives were radically changed. Even now, as the pastor of this
church, I just try to stay out of the way of God and let Him move on people's hearts.
That's what evangelism really is: sharing who Jesus is, not giving up,
and allowing God to move on the hearts of the people around you.

—George Rayburn, Senior Pastor, Pure Heart Church, Arizona

Just as someone helped you begin your journey with Jesus, our Lord offers you a unique opportunity to play this same role in the lives of others around you.

24

How do you see evidence of Jesus' words, "The harvest is plentiful but the workers are few," in the world around you?

Who are some people in your life who are "ripe for the harvest"— in other words, are ready to be presented with the gospel of Jesus Christ? What makes you believe that they are ready at this time?

Jesus said to his disciples, "The harvest is plentiful but the workers are few. Ask the Lord of the harvest, therefore, to send out workers into his harvest field."

MATTHEW 9:37–38

Do you remember a time when you were a "sheep without a shepherd"? How did Jesus come and rescue you?

Who are the "sheep without a shepherd" in your life—people who yet need to have an encounter with Christ? List the people God lays on your heart in each of the following areas, and then write a prayer, asking God to help you share his love with them in the next few weeks.

DAY 24

Family members (immediate or extended):
Friends:
Acquaintances (neighbors, kids' sports teams, school, and so forth):
Work colleagues:
People you meet just for fun (gym, hobbies, hangouts):

When Jesus saw the crowds,
he had compassion on them,
because they were harassed
and helpless, like sheep
without a shepherd.

MATTHEW 9:36

Today's Scripture Passage:

Reflections from my HEART:

I *Honor* who you are. (Praise God for something.)
I *Express* who I'm not. (Confess any known sin.)
I *Affirm* who I am in you. (How does God see you?)
I *Request* your will for me. (Ask God for something.)
I *Thank* you for what you've done. (Thank God for something.)

DAY 24

25

One important skill in sharing the gospel is the ability to see past someone's surface appearance to his or her heart, which holds real needs that Jesus is waiting to address.

In your opinion, what are the greatest needs a person can have? Explain the reasons behind your choices.

It has been said that it's hard to share the gospel with someone who is physically hungry or otherwise in a needy state. Why is it important to meet certain needs that people have before introducing them to what they need the most: the living water that only Jesus can provide?

Jesus said, "Whoever drinks the water I give him will never thirst. Indeed, the water I give him will become in him a spring of water welling up to eternal life."

JOHN 4:14

Who is the neediest person that you know? What are his or her needs? How might these needs help point the person to Christ?

What sorts of things did you need from Christ before you encountered him? How has he met these needs in your life?

How can you use this testimony to share Jesus, the real Need-Meeter, with others around you who do not yet know him?

Jesus said, "The Son of Man came to seek and to save what was lost."

LUKE 19:10

DAY
25

Today's Scripture Passage:

Reflections from my HEART:

I *Honor* who you are. (Praise God for something.)
I *Express* who I'm not. (Confess any known sin.)
I *Affirm* who I am in you. (How does God see you?)
I *Request* your will for me. (Ask God for something.)
I *Thank* you for what you've done. (Thank God for something.)

DAY
25

_____
_____
_____
_____
_____
_____
_____
_____
_____
_____
_____
_____
_____
_____
_____
_____
_____
_____

THE SKILL OF LISTENING
FOR NEEDS

READ JOHN 4:4–29.

With insight from the Holy Spirit, Jesus knew that the Samaritan woman had five husbands. The Holy Spirit may not give you such dramatic insight about strangers, but he does desire to help you discern the felt needs and real needs of people around you. You can learn to notice the broken places in people's lives. Sensitive questions and practical acts, such as giving and receiving water, can speak powerfully to people about your respect and concern for them. Most people are as thirsty for respect and kindness as the Samaritan woman was.

Jesus modeled how to discern a person's real needs. As you listen to the needs someone expresses, you can simply ask a few caring questions that invite her to share more of her heart with you. By listening well, you can draw her out further.

The Five R's of Listening help to keep a conversation going and create an atmosphere that draws someone out:

1. *Repeat what the person has shared with you.*
2. *Repeat his last sentence to encourage him to share more.*
3. *Return his comment with another question.*
4. *Respond with affirmation and gratitude for his willingness to share.*
5. *Renew your commitment to listen and pray for him.*

In the next few days, practice using these Five R's in conversation with the people around you. Then record your responses to the following questions.

Did the use of the Five R's enhance your conversation(s) in any way? If so, how?

What did you learn from these conversation(s)?

What will you do differently the next time?

26

Most of us come across unbelievers in the natural course of our lives. Simply opening our eyes to the people we encounter gives us many opportunities to share God's love.

Who are some of the unbelievers you encounter on a regular basis? What "common ground" can you establish with these people in order to become a witness to them?

When befriending non-believers, it is important to "keep your bearings in Christ" (See 1 Corinthians 9:21 the message.). What does this mean to you?

> Whatever a person is like, I try to find common ground with him so that he will let me tell him about Christ and let Christ save him. I do this to get the Gospel to them and also for the blessing I myself receive when I see them come to Christ.
>
> **1 CORINTHIANS 9:22–23 TLB**

Have you ever led anyone to Christ? Describe the experience.

What blessings did you receive from your involvement in this experience?

How can you go about building stronger relationships with non-believers?
List some practical ways you can do this in the next week.

DAY 26

We are Christ's ambassadors, as though God were making his appeal through us.
We implore you on Christ's behalf: Be reconciled to God. **2 CORINTHIANS 5:20**

_____

_____

_____

_____

_____

_____

_____

_____

_____

_____

_____

_____

_____

_____

_____

_____

_____

Today's Scripture Passage:

Reflections from my HEART:

I *Honor* who you are. (Praise God for something.)
I *Express* who I'm not. (Confess any known sin.)
I *Affirm* who I am in you. (How does God see you?)
I *Request* your will for me. (Ask God for something.)
I *Thank* you for what you've done. (Thank God for something.)

DAY 26

_____

_____

_____

_____

_____

_____

_____

_____

_____

_____

_____

_____

_____

27

Sharing our faith scares many Christians today.
But sharing our faith can be a natural part of life together.

What does it mean to "be wise" in our encounters with non-Christians?
Provide examples of wise and unwise actions in this context.

Describe a time when you made the most of an opportunity to witness
for the Lord. What was the result?

Be wise in the way you
act toward outsiders;
make the most of every
opportunity. Let your
conversation be always
full of grace, seasoned
with salt, so that you
may know how to
answer everyone.

—COLOSSIANS 4:5–6

Describe a time when you let an opportunity to witness go by. How did you feel afterward? What was the result?

What does it mean to have conversations that are "full of grace and seasoned with salt"? Describe a recent conversation you have had that might have met these criteria.

How would you handle an opportunity to speak about your faith? What are some of the things you would say? (If you don't know, turn to the next few pages to learn how to share your story with an unbeliever.)

Pray for us, that God may open a door for our message, so that we may proclaim the mystery of Christ. **COLOSSIANS 4:3**

DAY
27

One helpful tool in taking advantage of opportunities to witness is the ability to tell your personal story of faith in a way to which an outsider can relate. Others may question God's words in the Bible, but no one can discredit what he has done and is doing in your life. Use the following questions to help formulate the personal story of what Jesus has done for you.

What my life was like before Jesus

What circumstances or attitudes would an unbeliever identify with? What was most important to you? What substitute(s) for God did you use to find meaning in your life? (Substitutes include sports/fitness, success at work, marriage, children, sex, making money, drugs/alcohol, having fun, entertainment, popularity, hobbies, and so on.) If you've been a Christian since childhood, it may not be helpful for you to describe what you were like at, say, five years old. But at some point in your life, you've probably been tempted to lean on a substitute instead of on Jesus. Maybe you were tempted to find your self-worth in a perfect marriage and family, or maybe your career began to draw your love away from Jesus. Sinners trust Jesus partly because he admitted to being tempted in every way (Hebrews 4:15). If even Jesus was thoroughly tempted in ways sinners can identify with, the same is very likely true of you.

DAY 27

How I realized I needed Jesus

What significant steps led up to your conversion? What needs, hurts, or problems made you dissatisfied with the way you were living without God? (Choose a theme.) How did God get your attention? What motivated you? If you've been a Christian since childhood, describe a more recent temptation or a time of suffering when you needed Jesus.

DAY

27

How I committed my life to Jesus

What specifically did you do to step across the line? Where did it happen? What did you say in your prayer? Be specific. If you've been a Christian since childhood, describe what you did to turn to Jesus in that time of temptation or suffering. Be sure to include admitting your need for forgiveness, because this is something unbelievers rarely hear people admit.

DAY
27

The difference this choice has made in my life

What benefits have you experienced or felt? What problems have been resolved? How has Jesus helped you change for the better? How has he helped your relationships? Give a current example. If you've been a Christian since childhood, describe how God protected you, cared for you, and forgave you in your time of temptation or suffering. Also describe how this experience continues to affect your life.

DAY
27

Today's Scripture Passage:

Reflections from my HEART:

I *Honor* who you are. (Praise God for something.)
I *Express* who I'm not. (Confess any known sin.)
I *Affirm* who I am in you. (How does God see you?)
I *Request* your will for me. (Ask God for something.)
I *Thank* you for what you've done. (Thank God for something.)

DAY
27

Whether it's someone we've just met or a longtime friend, there comes a time when we must speak of what faith in Jesus Christ is all about.

28

How has knowing Christ brought hope into your life?

Name several people whom you know need to experience this same kind of hope.

Always be prepared to give an answer to everyone who asks you to give the reason for the hope that you have. But do this with gentleness and respect.

1 PETER 3:15

What does it mean to share the gospel with gentleness and respect? How have you seen this type of witness demonstrated?

Have you ever seen a "disrespectful" presentation of the gospel? Describe the situation. What was the result?

How have you "prepared yourself" to give an answer to those who ask you about Jesus? Do you feel prepared? How might you prepare yourself further?

DAY 28

The Lord is not slow in keeping his promise, as some understand slowness. He is patient with you, not wanting anyone to perish, but everyone to come to repentance.

2 PETER 3:9

Today's Scripture Passage:

Reflections from my HEART:

I *Honor* who you are. (Praise God for something.)
I *Express* who I'm not. (Confess any known sin.)
I *Affirm* who I am in you. (How does God see you?)
I *Request* your will for me. (Ask God for something.)
I *Thank* you for what you've done. (Thank God for something.)

29

A person's last words before going away are often the thoughts closest to his or her heart. Jesus' parting words encourage us to spread the good news throughout the world.

What does the phrase "all nations" mean to you? When, if ever, have you encountered someone from a different culture than your own?

These words of Jesus are also known as the "Great Commission." What feelings do the words cause you to experience? Why do you suppose you feel this way?

Jesus said, "Go and make disciples of all nations, baptizing them in the name of the Father and of the Son and of the Holy Spirit, teaching them to obey everything I have commanded you. And surely I am with you always, to the very end of the age."

MATTHEW 28:19–20

What do Jesus' words, "Surely I am with you always," mean to you in the context of being a witness for him?

In what creative ways could you widen your circle of love and embrace people from other cultures and even other continents?

Write a prayer for the nations of the earth, expressing God's heart and desire to see all peoples of the world turn to him.

> Jesus said, "You will receive power when the Holy Spirit comes on you; and you will be my witnesses in Jerusalem, and in all Judea and Samaria, and to the ends of the earth." **ACTS 1:8**

**DAY
29**

_____

_____

_____

_____

_____

_____

_____

_____

_____

_____

_____

_____

_____

_____

_____

_____

_____

_____

Today's Scripture Passage:

Reflections from my HEART:

I *Honor* who you are. (Praise God for something.)
I *Express* who I'm not. (Confess any known sin.)
I *Affirm* who I am in you. (How does God see you?)
I *Request* your will for me. (Ask God for something.)
I *Thank* you for what you've done. (Thank God for something.)

DAY
29

The way we formed our group was unique. My husband wanted to have "new" people

in the group—people we had not associated with nor who had been in any other

small groups. We asked a few people from church, but mostly we put out flyers to

our neighbors, because many of them are not Christians. And our group is growing.

But even more than that, the neighborhood notices when people are coming to and

leaving from our house, and so it has given us the opportunity to share with

our neighbors more than we ever thought it would! There is a curiosity factor there—

and we have become a lot closer to many of our neighbors in the process. Just by being

the light and by being an example—that's how you share and how you evangelize.

—Tim and Jenna

SURRENDERING YOUR LIFE
FOR GOD'S PLEASURE

WORSHIP

I would love to stride into church on a Sunday morning with the joy of surrender

welling up from my inner being. It rarely happens. More often than not, I've been driving

a carful of kids while combing their hair and insisting that they wolf down some breakfast.

I am frequently late, so I rush, slightly sweating, into the worship service. The first song

helps me begin to corral my thoughts and aim them in the general direction of God.

I have to decide to put everything else aside and make this time be about him.

The song lyrics remind me what my life is about—life together with my magnificent Lord.

By the third song, I'm aware that God is doing something in my heart. Peace fills me.

God's majesty transcends my life's chaotic details. I have become a worshiper.

—Denise

30

Worship is central to our life together with God. Worship must always begin with the attitude of our hearts toward him.

What characteristics of God most make you desire to worship him?

What does it mean to be a "living sacrifice"?

I urge you, brothers, in view of God's mercy, to offer your bodies as living sacrifices, holy and pleasing to God— this is your spiritual act of worship.

ROMANS 12:1

When you think of offering yourself to God in this way, what, if any, reservations do you have? What can you do to overcome these reservations?

With what forms of worship are you most comfortable?
With which forms might you be less comfortable? Why?

DAY 30

Come, let us bow down in worship, let us kneel before the LORD our Maker;

for he is our God and we are the people of his pasture, the flock under his care.

PSALM 95:6–7

Paul envisioned worship as an all-day-long surrender to the will of a merciful God. How do you worship God throughout the day?

In what new ways might God be calling you to worship him? How will you carry this out in the next week?

Shout for joy to the LORD, all the earth, worship the LORD with gladness; come before him with joyful songs. **PSALM 100:1–2**

DAY

30

Today's Scripture Passage:

Reflections from my HEART:

I *Honor* who you are. (Praise God for something.)
I *Express* who I'm not. (Confess any known sin.)
I *Affirm* who I am in you. (How does God see you?)
I *Request* your will for me. (Ask God for something.)
I *Thank* you for what you've done. (Thank God for something.)

DAY

30

_____

_____

_____

_____

_____

_____

_____

_____

_____

_____

_____

_____

_____

_____

_____

_____

_____

_____

31

Trusting God to run both the universe and our personal
lives is an essential step in the surrendered life.
We need to become convinced that he really is faithful
enough, powerful enough, and wise enough to do his job.

How has the Lord been great in your life? Why is he worthy of praise?

Do remembering God's acts of greatness in your life inspire you to
trust him any more?
Why or why not?

Great is the LORD and
most worthy of praise;
his greatness no one
can fathom.

PSALM 145:3

Have you ever doubted the greatness of God or been tempted to distrust him? What was the situation? How was it resolved?

What promises has the Lord fulfilled in your life?

What promises are you still waiting for him to fulfill?

DAY 31

The LORD is faithful to all his promises and loving toward all he has made… My mouth will speak in praise of the LORD. Let every creature praise his holy name for ever and ever. **PSALM 145:13, 21**

How has remembering God's great acts inspired you to worship him more fully?

Write a prayer of worship to the Lord, expressing your gratitude for the great things he has done and is doing in your life.

Praise the LORD, O my soul. O LORD my God, you are very great.

PSALM 104:1

DAY
31

Today's Scripture Passage:

Reflections from my HEART:

I *Honor* who you are. (Praise God for something.)
I *Express* who I'm not. (Confess any known sin.)
I *Affirm* who I am in you. (How does God see you?)
I *Request* your will for me. (Ask God for something.)
I *Thank* you for what you've done. (Thank God for something.)

DAY
31

There is a time for "forgetting what is behind and straining toward what is ahead" (Philippians 3:13), but first comes a decision to offer to God "what is behind." All of it—good and bad.

Have you ever wanted to share in the sufferings of Christ? Why is this such a strange attitude to have in our culture?

What "suffering" in your past is difficult for you to relinquish?

I want to know Christ and the power of his resurrection and the fellowship of sharing in his sufferings.

PHILIPPIANS 3:10

How might considering this suffering as a type of fellowship with Christ be helpful to you?

Surrendering the past can be a difficult thing to do.
How can keeping your eyes on the "prize" help you to "forget what is behind"?

DAY 32

Christ suffered for you, leaving you an example,
that you should follow in his steps. **1 PETER 2:21**

What is a beginning step you can take to surrender one area of your past? Some examples might include: writing a letter to God, writing a letter to someone who has hurt you, confiding in a pastor or close friend about past sins in your life and praying with them for forgiveness, or journaling a prayer of relinquishment here.

What will this step cost you, and what will be the rewards?

Forgetting what is behind and straining toward what is ahead,
I press on toward the goal to win the prize for which God has called me
heavenward in Christ Jesus. **PHILIPPIANS 3:13–14**

DAY
32

Today's Scripture Passage:

Reflections from my HEART:

I *Honor* who you are. (Praise God for something.)
I *Express* who I'm not. (Confess any known sin.)
I *Affirm* who I am in you. (How does God see you?)
I *Request* your will for me. (Ask God for something.)
I *Thank* you for what you've done. (Thank God for something.)

DAY
32

33

Hope is wanting and believing in something you don't have yet. And in that space between wanting and having, between the present and the future, lies a gap that you can fill with one of three things: despair, fear, or faith.

Is there anything in your life that you have been certain of, but couldn't see?

What are you hoping for at this time in your life?

Faith is being sure of what we hope for and certain of what we do not see.

HEBREWS 11:1

God invites you to surrender your hopes and dreams to him.
Which of the hopes you listed are difficult for you to turn over to him?

Why are these so difficult to relinquish?

Opening your heart and surrendering to God is an intimate act of worship.
Write a statement of worship to God, telling him of your desire to place
your ultimate hope in him.

DAY 33

Without faith it is impossible to please God, because anyone who comes to him
must believe that he exists and that he rewards those who earnestly seek him.

HEBREWS 11:6

_____

_____

_____

_____

_____

_____

_____

_____

_____

_____

_____

_____

_____

_____

_____

Today's Scripture Passage:

Reflections from my HEART:

I *Honor* who you are. (Praise God for something.)
I *Express* who I'm not. (Confess any known sin.)
I *Affirm* who I am in you. (How does God see you?)
I *Request* your will for me. (Ask God for something.)
I *Thank* you for what you've done. (Thank God for something.)

34

No matter whom we say we worship, we really worship whatever we think, deep down, gives us life.

How has God been a "spring of living water" to your life?

It is often hard to discern when we are worshiping something other than God, that is, "digging our own cistern." Some clues are where we spend our time and money, what we feel we can't live without, and to what we turn when we feel frustrated or empty.

Name some "broken cisterns" you have dug in your life.

"My people have committed two sins," declares the LORD "They have forsaken me, the spring of living water, and have dug their own cisterns, broken cisterns that cannot hold water."

JEREMIAH 2:13

What are some "broken cisterns" you are digging right now?
Why do these particular things appeal to your sense of worship?

How can you begin to return to God as your only source of living water?

Write a prayer of surrender to the Lord, asking him to help you relinquish your "broken cisterns" and turn only to him as your source in life.

As the deer pants for streams of water, so my soul pants for you, O God. My soul thirsts for God, for the living God. **PSALM 42:1–2**

DAY
34

Today's Scripture Passage:

Reflections from my HEART:

I *Honor* who you are. (Praise God for something.)
I *Express* who I'm not. (Confess any known sin.)
I *Affirm* who I am in you. (How does God see you?)
I *Request* your will for me. (Ask God for something.)
I *Thank* you for what you've done. (Thank God for something.)

DAY
34

35

Ultimately, to offer yourself as a living sacrifice to God is to say, "Here I am, Lord. My life belongs to you. Who would you like me to be?"

While Jesus prayed the words, "Father, into your hands I commit my spirit," at his death, we might pray them concerning our lives. In what ways might you commit your spirit to God?

Your entire life can be an act of worship to God. As you think about your life, look ahead to the day of your funeral. What would you like said about you in your eulogy, or what would you like to see inscribed on your tombstone?

Into your hands I commit my spirit; redeem me, O LORD, the God of truth.

PSALM 31:5

Why do you believe Paul could be glad and rejoice at the end of his life, even despite all of the hardships he had experienced?

Take a few moments and consider your life mission statement. Begin it with the words, "Here I am, Lord. Use me." Then write whatever you feel God wants you to do with the rest of your life. Finally, write a statement of commitment to follow him wherever he leads.

DAY 35

Even if I am being poured out like a drink offering on the sacrifice and service coming from your faith, I am glad and rejoice with all of you. **PHILIPPIANS 2:17**

Today's Scripture Passage:

Reflections from my HEART:

I *Honor* who you are. (Praise God for something.)
I *Express* who I'm not. (Confess any known sin.)
I *Affirm* who I am in you. (How does God see you?)
I *Request* your will for me. (Ask God for something.)
I *Thank* you for what you've done. (Thank God for something.)

_____
_____
_____
_____
_____
_____
_____
_____
_____
_____
_____
_____
_____
_____
_____
_____
_____

NEW TESTAMENT
READING PLAN

PURPOSE-DRIVEN LIFE HEALTH ASSESSMENT

	Just Beginning	Getting Going	Well Developed

CONNECTING WITH GOD'S FAMILY

I am deepening my understanding of and friendship with God in community with others — 1 2 3 4 5

I am growing in my ability both to share and to show my love to others — 1 2 3 4 5

I am willing to share my real needs for prayer and support from others — 1 2 3 4 5

I am resolving conflict constructively and am willing to forgive others — 1 2 3 4 5

CONNECTING Total _____

GROWING TO BE LIKE CHRIST

I have a growing relationship with God through regular time in the Bible and in prayer (spiritual habits) — 1 2 3 4 5

I am experiencing more of the characteristics of Jesus Christ (love, joy, peace, patience, kindness, self-control, etc.) in my life — 1 2 3 4 5

I am avoiding addictive behaviors (food, television, busyness, and the like) to meet my needs — 1 2 3 4 5

I am spending time with a Christian friend (spiritual partner) who celebrates and challenges my spiritual growth — 1 2 3 4 5

GROWING Total _____

DEVELOPING YOUR SHAPE TO SERVE OTHERS

I have discovered and am further developing my unique God-given shape for ministry — 1 2 3 4 5

I am regularly praying for God to show me opportunities to serve him and others — 1 2 3 4 5

I am serving in a regular (once a month or more) ministry in the church or community — 1 2 3 4 5

I am a team player in my small group by sharing some group role or responsibility — 1 2 3 4 5

DEVELOPING Total_____

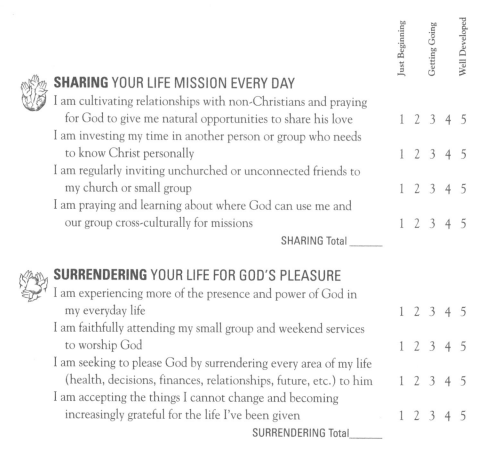

SHARING YOUR LIFE MISSION EVERY DAY

	Just Beginning	Getting Going	Well Developed

I am cultivating relationships with non-Christians and praying
for God to give me natural opportunities to share his love   1   2   3   4   5

I am investing my time in another person or group who needs
to know Christ personally   1   2   3   4   5

I am regularly inviting unchurched or unconnected friends to
my church or small group   1   2   3   4   5

I am praying and learning about where God can use me and
our group cross-culturally for missions   1   2   3   4   5

SHARING Total _____

SURRENDERING YOUR LIFE FOR GOD'S PLEASURE

I am experiencing more of the presence and power of God in
my everyday life   1   2   3   4   5

I am faithfully attending my small group and weekend services
to worship God   1   2   3   4   5

I am seeking to please God by surrendering every area of my life
(health, decisions, finances, relationships, future, etc.) to him   1   2   3   4   5

I am accepting the things I cannot change and becoming
increasingly grateful for the life I've been given   1   2   3   4   5

SURRENDERING Total_____

Total your scores for each purpose, and place them on the chart below. Reassess
your progress at the end of thirty days. Be sure to select your spiritual partner and
the one area in which you'd like to make progress over the next thirty days.

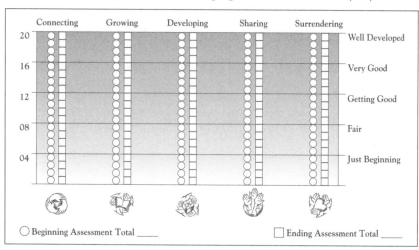

PURPOSE-DRIVEN LIFE HEALTH PLAN

My Name _____ Date _____

My Spiritual Partner _____ Date _____

Possibilities	Plan
	(make one goal for each area)

CONNECTING WITH GOD'S FAMILY
Hebrews 10:24 – 25; Ephesians 2:19
How can I deepen my relationships with others?

- Attend my group more faithfully

- Schedule lunch with a group member

- Begin praying for a spiritual mentor

WHO is/are my shepherd(s)?

NAME: _____

GROWING TO BE LIKE CHRIST
Colossians 1:28; Ephesians 4:15
How can I grow to be like Christ?

- Commit to personal time with God three days a week

- Ask a friend for devotional accountability

- Begin journaling my prayers

WHAT is my Spiritual Health Plan?

RENEWAL DATE: _____

DEVELOPING YOUR SHAPE TO SERVE OTHERS
Ephesians 4:11 – 13; 1 Corinthians 12:7; 1 Peter 3:10
How can I develop my shape for ministry?

- Begin praying for a personal ministry

- Attend a gift discovery class

- Serve together at a church event or in the community

WHERE am I serving others?

MINISTRY: _____

SHARING YOUR LIFE MISSION EVERY DAY
Matthew 28:18 – 20; Acts 20:24
How can I share my faith every day?

- Start meeting for lunch with a seeker friend

- Invite a non-Christian relative to church

- Pray for and support an overseas missionary

WHEN am I sharing my life mission?

TIME: _____

SURRENDERING YOUR LIFE FOR GOD'S PLEASURE
How can I surrender my life for God's pleasure?

- Submit one area to God

- Be honest about my struggle and hurt

- Buy a music CD for worship in my car and in the group

HOW am I surrendering my life today?

AREA: _____

SHAPE
WORKSHEET

God has designed you with a unique SHAPE. Your SHAPE enables you to serve God in ways no other person can. It makes you irreplaceable. If you know your SHAPE, you'll have many clues about the service to which God is calling you. Discerning God's will for your life becomes much easier.

This worksheet will help you discover and develop your SHAPE. By the end of session 6, you will have all five areas filled out. You will also have feedback from your group members that affirms what they see in you for each area. Use this worksheet as a guideline for choosing ministry both inside and outside your group.

Spiritual Gifts

- ☐ Preaching
- ☐ Evangelism
- ☐ Discernment
- ☐ Apostle
- ☐ Teaching
- ☐ Encouragement
- ☐ Wisdom
- ☐ Missions
- ☐ Service
- ☐ Mercy
- ☐ Hospitality
- ☐ Pastoring
- ☐ Giving
- ☐ Intercession
- ☐ Music
- ☐ Arts and Crafts
- ☐ Healing
- ☐ Miracles
- ☐ Leadership
- ☐ Administration
- ☐ Faith

Heart — I Love to

- ☐ design/develop
- ☐ pioneer
- ☐ organize
- ☐ operate/maintain
- ☐ serve/help
- ☐ acquire/possess
- ☐ excel
- ☐ perform
- ☐ improve
- ☐ repair
- ☐ lead/be in charge
- ☐ persevere
- ☐ follow the rules
- ☐ prevail
- ☐ influence

Abilities

- [ ] Entertaining
- [ ] Recruiting
- [ ] Interviewing
- [ ] Researching
- [ ] Artistic/Graphics
- [ ] Evaluating
- [ ] Planning
- [ ] Managing
- [ ] Counseling
- [ ] Teaching
- [ ] Writing/Editing
- [ ] Promoting
- [ ] Repairing
- [ ] Feeding
- [ ] Recall
- [ ] Mechanical Operating
- [ ] Resourceful
- [ ] Counting/Classifying
- [ ] Public Relations
- [ ] Welcoming
- [ ] Composing
- [ ] Landscaping
- [ ] Arts and Crafts
- [ ] Decorating
- [ ] Musical
- [ ] _____
- [ ] _____

Experiences

- [ ] Spiritual:

- [ ] Painful:

- [ ] Education:

- [ ] Work:

- [ ] Ministry:

Personality

	Hi	Lo	Lo	Hi	
Introverted	[ ]	[ ]	[ ]	[ ]	Extroverted
Variety	[ ]	[ ]	[ ]	[ ]	Routine
Self-Expressive	[ ]	[ ]	[ ]	[ ]	Self-Controlled
Competitive	[ ]	[ ]	[ ]	[ ]	Cooperative

KEY VERSES
TO MEMORIZE

Matthew 5:8	2 Timothy 1:6
Ephesians 4:32	Genesis 50:20
Proverbs 27:17	Matthew 19:26
James 5:16	John 3:16
Proverbs 25:11	Luke 19:10
Psalm 9:1	2 Corinthians 5:20
Matthew 6:33	Colossians 4:5
Ephesians 3:16–17	2 Peter 3:9
Luke 10:41–42	Matthew 28:19–20
Psalm 46:10	Romans 12:1
2 Timothy 2:15	Psalm 145:3
James 1:2–3	Psalm 139:16
Psalm 139:14	Hebrews 11:6
Mark 10:43	Philippians 3:7
1 Peter 4:10	Psalm 31:5

At Inspirio we love to hear from you—your
stories, your feedback,
and your product ideas.
Please send your comments to us
by way of e-mail at
icares@zondervan.com
or to the address below:

inspirio

Attn: Inspirio Cares
5300 Patterson Avenue SE
Grand Rapids, MI 49530

If you would like further information
about Inspirio and the products we
create please visit us at:
www.inspiriogifts.com

Thank you and God bless!